Unit 2

Animal Discoveries

Contents

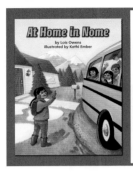

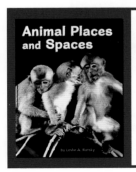

At Home in Nome

by Lois Owens
illustrated by Kathi Ember

May 9

I am in Nome. My family just moved here. I have a lot to tell. I have a big bed and not just a cot. I have a new school, too. I am scared because I do not know the kids. I hope they like me. I hope I make a lot of friends.

May 11

It is May, but it is still cold! Do not take off your hat. It is not hot like it is back home.

There were fox prints in the mud. Dad took a picture to take home.

May 15

Mom drove me to school. Back home I rode my bike. I like to ride.

All the kids spoke to me! I like my class. I made lots of friends. I will get to ride a big bus to school, too!

4

May 23

There are crab and cod in Nome.
I am glad I like cod. Yum! Yum!
Mom will make crab on the stove.
I hope I like it!

May 30

I will like making a trip back
home some time. I miss my pals.
I miss sitting in the sun. I miss
running in the grass. I miss riding a
bike. But for now, I am glad to have
a home in Nome!

Duke and Bud's Run

by Leslie A. Rotsky
illustrated by Steven Mach

On a June day, Bud the hare
was sitting in the hot sun. "I bet
I can win any race," Bud yelled.
Bud could hop and run for miles
and miles and miles. Bud was as
fast as a man on a bike.

Duke the tortoise was sitting in the hot sun, too. He was up on a big hill in a tub of mud. Duke yelled to Bud, "I will race you. And I bet I will win because I am not rude like you. It is not wise to brag."

"Duke, you are funny," Bud said,
"I have won five times. You will
not win. I am fast! I am the best!"

"Yes, you and I should race,"
Duke said. "You are fast, but I am
wise. Run and change, Bud."

10

Duke and Bud came to race at six. Bud had a big jug of water and a fan. Duke just had a bit of a smile.

Duke and Bud's friends came in time to see their race and cheer.

"Look," said Cal the cub. "I will tell you the rules. I will open the gate and hit a bell. You must run on the grass and not in the mud. Do not stop. To win, run up the hill and get to the red line.

12

Duke and Bud got set.
"Do not trip and fall," joked Bud.
"I hope you do well," said Duke.
Cal opened the gate. Bud ran off. He was fast. You could not spot him. Duke took his time, but he did not stop.

13

Bud stopped. He sat in the grass and hummed a tune. He sipped from his red jug. Bud even took a nap.

Duke did not go fast, but he did not stop. Bud woke up too late. Duke got to the red line and won! Bud was mad.

Animal Places and Spaces

and Spaces

by Leslie A. Rotsky

Animals make nice homes in many places and spaces.

This big wolf's home is a cave. The wolf has cubs in the cave. The cubs are safe there. Big cats and bats make fine homes in big caves too.

A mole lodges in the ground.
It digs and digs making a hole it
uses as its home. In a hole a mole
gets food like grubs. A mole will
pop straight out of a hole and show
its face, but likes it best under the
ground. It is safe there.

What animal makes a fine home in a huge tree? A squirrel lives in a tree. It can pull nuts off the tree. A squirrel stuffs nuts in its face making it bulge. A tree is a safe place to hide and play.

A nest is a home for a bird. Birds use twigs, grass, and mud to make nests. Some nests look like cups. In a nest, birds can dodge enemies. Some birds will not budge if they are sitting on eggs. Birds can reuse a nest or make a new nest.

A spider makes its home in a web. It spins a web. A web can get big. It is made out of silk. A web looks like lace you buy. You can dislike big spiders, but they trap bad bugs in their webs. Spiders dine on bugs.

Lots of animals make homes in water. Crabs and fish live in water almost as blue as the sky. Fish swim and dive in big waves. Some crabs move on and change homes. Some crabs wash up in hot sand.

On these pages
you saw homes
in lots of places
and spaces. Caves,
nests, and webs
make nice homes.

Could an animal make a home
in your home? Yes, a cage can
make a nice home for some pets.
Get a pet and make a home!

Animal	Home
wolf, cat, bat	cave
mole	hole
squirrel	tree
bird	nest
spider	web
crab, fish	water
pet	cage

Baby Watch

by Leslie A. Rotsky

Some baby animals can hatch from an egg. Some baby animals look like mom and dad. Some do not. These playful pups look like mom. Dog moms can have seven or eight pups at a time.

Early on, this baby will try to walk. Its long, thin legs shake, but it will start to run in just a bit. When this baby has to rest, it can take a nap while it is standing up.

This isn't a little baby. It is huge!
What can this big baby learn? It
can learn to use its long trunk. It
can grab food, get wet, and hang
on to a pal. When an elephant gets
hot, it is time for a long mud bath.
It likes that!

Some animal moms watch their babies. A little fish can make a nice lunch for a big fish. These baby fish swim close to mom. If one is in danger, it can rush and swim in to mom's mouth. It is safe there.

This cat is not in a big cage. Can you spot its face? Cubs hide while mom gets food. Mom can not chat with the cubs on a phone, but she can moan to get them. Cubs like running and playing, just like kids!

Mrs. Sprig's Spring Flowers

by Leslie A. Rotsky
illustrated by Steven Mach

"When can I help?"
Chip asked.

"It is time, Chip," Mrs. Sprig
spoke up. "Move that dirt pile by
those far shrubs into this field."

Thad wished he could help, but
he was just too little.

"It is time to dig holes in this spot," said Mrs. Sprig with a smile.

Chip was strong. Chip dug and dug. He made a long strip of holes. Then Chip stopped to scratch his leg.

Thad just sat and watched.

"Next you must get this dirt wet," said Mrs. Sprig.

Chip grabbed a big hose. It was fun making water splish and splash until the dirt was ready. It looked like mud.

Thad *really* wished he could help.

Mrs. Sprig had packs of strange little seeds. "I like lots and lots of spring flowers," she said.

"Thad, you are just the right size for this fun job. Shake seeds in the holes just like this," Mrs. Sprig said.

Thad was thrilled to pitch in.
Mrs. Sprig said, "This seed will
grow into a blue flower. It will
need light and water. Then you
will see leaves spring up. This seed
will grow into a big orange
and white flower."

Bird stopped to sit and chat.
"Bird, it is nice that you came.
I like your red hat," said Mrs. Sprig.
"We are done planting. We will
scrub up and change. Then you
can have pie with us."

Mrs. Sprig, Chip, Thad, and Bird sat in the sun and had pie. Chip ate a little slice, and Thad ate a big slice!

Mrs. Sprig sat back and pictured a flowerbed filled with lots and lots of spring flowers.

Unit 2: Animal Discovery

to use with *A Visit to the Desert*   **WORD COUNT: 210**

DECODABLE WORDS

Target Phonics Elements

> **short *o***
>> cod, cot, hot, fox, lot, lots, Mom, not, on
>
> **Long *o*: *o_e***
>> home, Nome, hope, drove, rode, spoke, stove

HIGH-FREQUENCY WORDS

> because, cold, family, friends, have, know, off, picture, school, took
>
> **Review:** a, all, and, are, do, go, here, like, me, moved, my, new, of, show, some, the, there, they, to, too, were, your

STORY WORDS

> May, back, scared

37

to use with *The Boy Who Cried Wolf*　　　　　**WORD COUNT: 313**

DECODABLE WORDS

Target Phonics Elements

Short *u*

Bud, but, funny, hummed, jug, just, must, run, sun, up

Long *u: u_e*

cute, June, Duke, rude, rules, tune

HIGH-FREQUENCY WORDS

cheer, change, fall, five, look, open, should, their, won, yes

Review: any, are, because, could, do, even, for, funny, have, he, of, open, said, see, the, to, too, took, was, water, you

STORY WORDS

day, hare, race, tortoise

to use with *A Prairie Guard Dog*

WORD COUNT: 330

DECODABLE WORDS

Target Phonics Elements

Soft *c*

face, lace, nice, place, places, spaces

Soft *g: dge*

budge, dodge, lodges

Soft *g: lge*

bulge

Soft *g: ge*

huge, pages, cage

Soft *g: nge*

range, change

HIGH-FREQUENCY WORDS

almost, buy, food, out, pull, saw, sky, straight, under, wash

Review: are, change, could, do, for, from, here, look, move, new, of, or, open, play, show, some, the, their, there, they, this, to, too, water, what, you, your

STORY WORDS

animal(s), birds, blue, enemies, fish, ground, live(s), squirrel, spiders, these, tree

39

to use with *Eagles and Eaglets*   **WORD COUNT: 222**

DECODABLE WORDS

Target Phonics Elements

Consonant Digraph ch:

chat, lunch

Consonant Digraph tch:

hatch, watch

Consonant Digraph sh:

fish, rush, shake

Consonant Digraphs ph:

elephant, phone

Consonant Digraph th:

that, the, their, them, there, these, they, thin, this

Consonant Digraph ng:

long, hang

Consonant Digraph wh:

what, when, while

Suffixes -ful, -less

playful, helpless

HIGH-FREQUENCY WORDS

baby, early, eight, isn't, learn, seven, start, these, try, walk

Review: by, do, food, for, from, have, little, look, one, or, play, she, some, the, their, there, they, to, you

STORY WORDS

animal(s), babies, be, born, danger, elephant, moan, mouth

to use with *Cats and Mittens, Desert Camels* **WORD COUNT: 288**

DECODABLE WORDS

Target Phonics Elements

3-letter Blends:

scr scratch, scrub

shr shrubs

spl splash, splish

spr Sprig, Sprig's, spring

str strip, strong, strange

thr thrilled

HIGH-FREQUENCY WORDS

bird, far, field, flower, grow, leaves, light, orange, ready, until

Review: are, by, could, done, for, have, he, into, little, looked, move, of, pictured, right, said, see, she, the, to, too, was, water, you

STORY WORDS

dirt, need, pie, really, seed(s), we

HIGH-FREQUENCY WORDS TAUGHT TO DATE

Grade K	Grade I				Grade 2	
a	about	early	minutes	some	all	play
and	across	eat	more	soon	and	put
are	after	eight	mother	sound	another	right
can	again	enough	move	straight	any	said
do	against	every	never	sure	are	says
for	air	eyes	new	their	ball	see
go	all	fall	no	then	blue	she
has	along	father	not	there	both	show
have	also	find	nothing	they	boy	small
he	always	four	now	thought	by	some
here	another	friends	of	three	could	sounds
I	any	from	old	through	do	the
is	around	full	once	today	done	there
like	away	funny	one	together	even	they
little	ball	girl	only	too	find	this
look	be	give	open	two	for	to
me	because	goes	or	under	funny	too
my	been	gone	orange	until	girl	understands
play	before	good	other	up	go	want
said	begin	great	our	upon	goes	was
see	below	grew	out	use	green	water
she	better	head	over	very	has	were
the	blue	help	people	walked	he	what
this	boy	her	place	want	help	where
to	brought	house	poor	warm	here	why
was	build	how	pretty	water	how	work
we	buy	instead	pull	way	into	year
what	by	into	put	were	like	yellow
where	call	it	ride	who	little	you
with	carry	jump	run	why	me	your
you	certain	knew	saw	work	move	
	change	know	says	would	my	
	climbed	laugh	school	write	new	
	come	learn	searching	yellow	now	
	could	live	should	your	number	
	does	love	shout		of	
	done	make	show		on	
	down	many	so		one	
					or	
					other	

DECODING SKILLS TAUGHT TO DATE

CVC letter patterns; short *a*; consonants *b, c, ck, f, g, h, k, l, m, n, p, r, s, t, v*; inflectional ending *-s* (plurals, verbs); short *i*; consonants *d, j, qu, w, x, y, z*; double final consonants; *l* blends; possessives with *'s*; end blends; short *o*; inflectional ending *-ed*; short *e*; contractions with *n't*; *s* blends; *r* blends; inflectional ending *-ing*; short *u*; contractions with *'s*; digraphs *sh, th, ng*; compound words; long *a (a_e)*, inflectional ending *-ed* (drop final *e*); long *i (i_e)*; soft *c, g, -dge*; digraphs *ch, -tch, wh-, ph*; inflectional ending *-es* (no change to base word); long *e (e_e)*, long *o (o_e)*, long *u (u_e)*; silent letters *gn, kn, wr*; 3-letter blends *scr-, spl-, spr-, str-*; inflectional endings *-ed, -ing* (double final consonant); long *a (ai, ay)*; inflectional endings *-er, -est*; long *e (e, ea, ee, ie)*; *e* at the end of long *e* words; long *o (o, oa, oe, ow)*; 2-syllable words; long *i (i, ie, igh, y)*; 2-syllable inflectional endings (changing *y* to *ie*); long *e (ey, y)*; inflectional ending *-ed* (verbs; change *y* to *i*); *r*-controlled vowel /ûr/*er, ir, ur*; inflectional endings *-er, -est* (drop final *e*); *r*-controlled vowel /är/ *ar*; abbreviations Mr., Mrs., Dr.; *r*-controlled vowel /ôr/*or, oar, ore; ea* as short *e*; diphthong /ou/ *ou, ow*; final *e* (mouse, house); diphthong /oi/*oi, oy*; prefixes *re-, un-*; variant vowels /ù/*oo*, /ü/*oo, ew, ue, u_e, ou*; possessives; variant vowel /ô/*a, au, aw, augh*; singular and plural possessive pronouns; 2-syllable words; *r*-controlled vowel /âr/*air, are, ear*; contractions; open syllables; closed syllables; final stable syllables; vowel digraph syllables; *r*-controlled vowel syllables; vowel diphthong syllables; short *a, e, i, o, u*; consonant blends *dr, sl, sk, sp, st*; consonant digraphs *ch, -tch, sh, th, wh, ph*; long *a (a_e), i (i_e), o (o_e), u (u_e)*; soft *c* and *g*